• MUSIC •
Jazz and Blues

Nicolas Brasch

Smart Apple Media

This edition first published in 2005 in the United States of America by
Smart Apple Media.

Smart Apple Media
1980 Lookout Drive
North Mankato
Minnesota 56003

Library of Congress Cataloging-in-Publication Data

Brasch, Nicolas.
    Jazz and blues / by Nicolas Brasch.
    p. cm. — (Music)
    Includes index.
    ISBN 1-58340-548-8 (alk. paper)
    1. Jazz—History and criticism—Juvenile literature. 2. Blues
(Music)—History and criticism—Juvenile literature. I. Title.

    ML3506.B73 2004
    781.65—dc22   2004041602

First Edition
9 8 7 6 5 4 3 2 1

First published in 2003 by
MACMILLAN EDUCATION AUSTRALIA PTY LTD
627 Chapel Street, South Yarra 3141

Associated companies and representatives throughout the world.

Project management by Elm Grove Press
Edited by Helen Duffy
Text design by Judith Summerfeldt Grace
Cover design by Judith Summerfeldt Grace
Photo research by Helen Duffy and Ingrid Ohlsson

Printed in China

Acknowledgements

The author and the publisher are grateful to the following for
permission to reproduce copyright material.

Cover photographs: Photodisc (musical instruments); Bruce Postle
(left, drummer, Wilson Pickett blues band, Melbourne International
Blues Festival, 2003, right, Ray Charles, Melbourne International
Blues Festival, 2003).

Text photographs: Photodisc (musical instruments), pp. 10, 11, 24, 25;
Bruce Postle, pp. 1(bottom left, John Mayall and the Bluesbreakers,
Melbourne International Blues Festival, 2003), 1 (bottom right,
trombone player, Wilson Pickett blues band, Melbourne International
Blues Festival, 2003), 3 (top and second top, guitarist and saxophonist,
Wilson Pickett blues band, Melbourne International Blues Festival,
2003), 3 (third top, piano accordion player, New Zealand's Ortiz
Funeral Directors jazz band, Melbourne Jazz Festival, 2003), 3 (bottom,
James Morrison), 4 (from the collection in the Louvre, Paris), 5
(saxophonist, Wilson Pickett blues band, Melbourne International
Blues Festival, 2003), 8 (Acker Bilk, Brisbane Town Hall, 1968), 9
(James Morrison), 15 (bottom, Cleo Laine), 16, 19 (scene from musical
Hello Dolly, State Theatre, Melbourne, 1994), 20 (piano accordion
player, New Zealand's Ortiz Funeral Directors jazz band, Melbourne
Jazz Festival, 2003), 21 (Ray Charles, Melbourne International
Blues Festival, 2003), 23 (Brownie McGhee and Sonny Terry);
Redferns Music Picture Library, pp. 6 (copyright Michael Ochs
Archives/Redferns), 7 (Max Jones Files/Redferns), 12 (copyright
David Redfern/Redferns), 13 (copyright Ebet Roberts/Redferns),
14 (copyright David Redfern/Redferns), 15 (top, copyright
Gerrit Schilp/Redferns), 17 (copyright Bill Willoughby/Redferns),
18 (copyright David Redfern/Redferns), 27 (copyright Michael Ochs
Archives/Redferns), 28 (copyright Michael Ochs Archives/Redferns),
29 (copyright Harry Herd/Redferns).

While every care has been taken to trace and acknowledge copyright,
the publisher tenders their apologies for any accidental infringement
where copyright has proved untraceable. Where the attempt has been
unsuccessful, the publisher welcomes information that would redress
the situation.

Contents

Understanding Music   4

Jazz Music   5

    History of Jazz Music   6

    Instruments of Jazz Music   10

    Great Jazz Performers   12

    Great Jazz Compositions   16

Blues Music   20

    History of Blues Music   22

    Instruments of Blues Music   24

    Great Blues Performers   26

    Great Blues Compositions   30

Glossary   31

Index   32

Glossary
When a word is printed in **bold** you can find its meaning in the Glossary on page 31.

Understanding Music

Music has been enjoyed since ancient times.

Music is the arrangement and performance of a combination of sounds that are created by the human voice or by instruments. The ability to turn sounds into music or to create sounds that do not come naturally is something that only humans can do.

The desire to make music is common among all people. It helps us to communicate ideas or emotions and to understand our surroundings and way of life, as well as that of others.

Since ancient times, even isolated communities developed their own forms of music. Different groups used different techniques and instruments to create their own musical sounds.

Music is a creative art form. It also plays an important role in other art forms. Dance and some forms of theater use music to support the action on stage and to help create mood. Music also helps to create atmosphere in films and many television programs.

Music has its own written language, or **score**, made up of symbols and notes. Different musical notes are used to indicate the length of a sound. Notes are represented by the letters A, B, C, D, E, F, and G. These letters or notes are marked on a stave, which is a set of five parallel lines. The position of a note on the stave indicates whether the note is high or low.

Some of the most well-known types of music are:

- classical
- opera
- jazz
- blues
- folk
- country
- reggae
- pop
- rock

This book is about jazz and blues music.

Main Elements of Music

The main elements of all music are:

dynamics the variation in volume (from loud to soft)

pitch the depth of a sound (whether it is "high" or "low")

rhythm the general pattern or movement of a piece of music, which is created by the length of time between each beat

timbre the tonal quality of a sound

tonality the use of keys in music

Important Musical Terms

chord a combination of two or more musical notes played at the same time

harmony a specific chord or a series of chords

melody a series of musical sounds of different pitch (when you hum the tune of a song, you are usually humming the melody)

texture the thickness of a sound

Jazz Music

Jazz music was developed by African-Americans in the United States in the late 1800s. It has four main characteristics. These are its snappy, swinging rhythm, its emphasis on the music more than the **lyrics**, or words, and most important of all, its use of **improvization** and **syncopation**.

Swinging Rhythm

The swinging rhythm of jazz is created by musicians who move very quickly from one musical note to the next.

Emphasis on Music

In jazz, the music plays a more important role than the lyrics. Many jazz compositions are **instrumentals**.

Improvization

Improvization is the composing of music on the spur of the moment or without preparation. Musicians make up the music as they go along, and the musical notes are not written down. Many jazz songs are created in this way.

Syncopation

Syncopation is the stressing of beats that are not normally emphasized or that are usually heard in the background. This changes regular musical patterns.

Jazz is a group effort, performed by musicians playing different instruments. Some compositions include a **solo** piece. The greatest jazz artists—past and present—are always backed by other musicians.

History of Jazz Music

Great Ragtime Artists

Scott Joplin (1868–1917)

Ben Harney (1871–1938)

Tom Turpin (1873–1922)

Joseph Lamb (1877–1960)

Eubie Blake (1881–1983)

James Scott (1885–1938)

Artie Matthews (1888–1958)

Scott Joplin

The timeline gives some important jazz events from the 1890s to the 1920s.

Jazz is a distinctly American form of music. It developed in African-American communities within the United States, and it tells the story of their struggle for acceptance and equality.

Origins of Jazz

From the early 1600s, slaves were brought to the United States against their will from Africa, to work on the cotton plantations. They sang and made music as they lived and toiled. They were banned from using drums for fear they would send secret sound messages from one plantation to another. To compensate, the slaves **improvized** by beating parts of their bodies or other instruments to provide the beat. The government stopped slavery in 1863.

Ragtime

By the end of the 1800s, the music of the plantations was being performed in the clubs of the major southern cities. The style that became particularly popular in the late 1890s and early 1900s was ragtime. This was a fast-paced, syncopated style of music played on the piano.

The master of ragtime was a pianist named Scott Joplin. His tunes became known all the way from Texas to New York City, and his success encouraged many other African-Americans to start playing.

1895	1897	1899	1900	1902	1906	1907	1908	1909
Buddy Bolden begins playing the cornet	Tom Turpin publishes "Harlem Rag"	Scott Joplin has huge hit with "Maple Leaf Rag," and the sheet music sells an incredible 75,000 copies	Tom Turpin opens a cafe in St. Louis that becomes the meeting place for ragtime performers	Scott Joplin publishes "The Entertainer," which in 1973 becomes the theme music for the film *The Sting*	"Jelly Roll" Morton composes "King Porter Stomp"	Jazz founder Buddy Bolden is sent to a mental hospital and dies there in 1931	French classical music composer Debussy includes elements of ragtime in a piano suite	Ragtime music sales are so high that piano manufacturers find it hard to keep up with the demand for new pianos

1890s   *1900–1909*

New Orleans Jazz

Buddy Bolden is generally named as the "founder of jazz." He started playing the cornet in the 1890s, and his live performances in the city of New Orleans attracted musicians from all over town. By 1900, African-American musicians in New Orleans were playing a style of music that had few musical rules. It became known as New Orleans jazz (or traditional or Dixieland jazz). It was a mixture of ragtime, blues, and marching music.

The popularity of jazz spread quickly across the United States as New Orleans jazz musicians got onto trains and headed for clubs from New York to San Francisco.

Hot Jazz

The 1920s saw the rapid development across America of several different jazz styles. In New Orleans, jazz legend Louis Armstrong invented so-called hot jazz, which featured an improvized solo that led to a "hot" climax.

Chicago Style

The city of Chicago attracted many highly talented musicians, who developed a style of jazz that was strong on harmony. It required a level of expertise that was well above other jazz forms of the time.

Boogie Woogie

Another popular jazz style was the boogie woogie. The piano was the main instrument. The pianist played the **bass** part of the tune with the left hand and the melody with the right hand.

Great New Orleans Jazz Artists

Buddy Bolden (1877–1931)
King Oliver (1885–1938)
Kid Ory (1886–1973)
Freddie Keppard (1890–1933)
"Jelly Roll" Morton (1890–1941)
Johnny Dodds (1892–1940)
Sidney Bechet (1897–1959)
Louis Armstrong (1900–1971)

New Orleans musician "Jelly Roll" Morton had his own band called the Red Hot Peppers. "Jelly Roll" is seen here playing the piano.

1911	1913	1915	1917	1924
Clarinet player Sidney Bechet earns a name for his new and exciting playing	The word "jazz" is used in a newspaper article for the first time	"Jelly Roll" Morton publishes "Jelly Roll Blues," the first genuine jazz song to appear in print	The Original Dixieland Jazz Band takes jazz from New Orleans to New York, with great success	Louis Armstrong leaves King Oliver's Band to set up his own band

Swing

In the 1930s, swing became the most popular form of jazz. It was played by large bands or orchestras, with the brass section dominant. It was great music to dance to, and band leaders such as Glen Miller and Benny Goodman helped make it popular with non-African American audiences. Swing songs regularly topped the music charts.

Kansas City Style

The 1930s also saw a slower style of jazz develop in Kansas City. It combined elements of swing with the soulful blues music that was very popular at the time.

Be-bop

In the 1940s, a form of jazz called be-bop developed in New York. The music was more complex and made more use of improvization, particularly by solo performers. It was the first style of jazz created to listen to, rather than dance to, and it marked the beginning of the modern jazz era.

The 1950s

In the mid-1950s, rock and roll replaced jazz as the most popular form of music. The wild antics of Elvis Presley, Little Richard, and Chuck Berry held more appeal than the beat of jazz musicians. As a result, not many jazz songs after the 1950s appeared on the top of the music charts.

This was not only due to rock and roll. It was also because modern jazz was not as **commercial** as the earlier forms of jazz. However, the changing music scene did not stop jazz artists from developing new styles of jazz.

Acker Bilk, a clarinettist, has been one of Britain's biggest jazz stars since the mid-1950s.

The timeline gives some important jazz events from the 1930s to the 1990s and beyond.

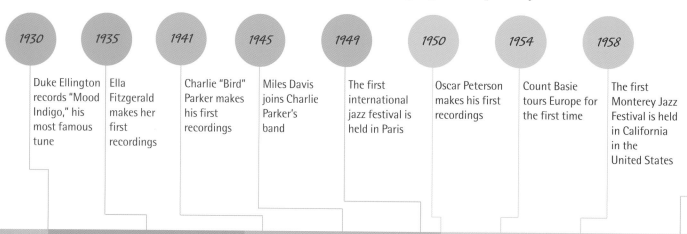

1930	1935	1941	1945	1949	1950	1954	1958
Duke Ellington records "Mood Indigo," his most famous tune	Ella Fitzgerald makes her first recordings	Charlie "Bird" Parker makes his first recordings	Miles Davis joins Charlie Parker's band	The first international jazz festival is held in Paris	Oscar Peterson makes his first recordings	Count Basie tours Europe for the first time	The first Monterey Jazz Festival is held in California in the United States

1930s   1940s   1950s

Modern Jazz

The term "modern jazz" applies to all forms of jazz developed since the 1950s. It is characterized by **experimentation** and radical improvization.

Cool Jazz

Cool jazz developed in the 1950s and combined be-bop and swing. While be-bop emphasized solo improvizations, cool jazz aimed to bring the musicians together again. The music was more important than the emotion.

Bossa Nova

Bossa nova combined elements of jazz with samba music from Brazil. The main instrument was the guitar. The most famous bossa nova performers were Joao Gilberto, Antonio Carlos Jobim, and Stan Getz.

Free Jazz

In the 1960s, music known as free jazz allowed the musicians to do just about anything they wanted. This total freedom of expression was not so popular with jazz fans.

Fusion

In the 1970s, several jazz musicians combined elements of traditional jazz with rock music. This music style became known as fusion and it influenced the sound of both jazz and rock. Fusion is the most recent jazz form.

Since the 1970s, the jazz scene has focused on **revivals** of earlier jazz styles. Jazz is still popular, but it is unlikely ever to recapture the glory days of the swing era.

James Morrison is Australia's greatest horn player of the modern jazz era.

1962	1967	1973	1978	1984	1995	2000
The bossa nova craze is at its peak	The first Montreaux Jazz Festival is held in Switzerland	Ragtime reappears on the scene when Scott Joplin's "The Entertainer" is used as the theme music for the hit film *The Sting*	U.S. President Jimmy Carter hosts a jazz concert at the White House, which features great jazz performers	A jazz band from the Soviet Union, the Ganelin Trio, tours Britain	Swing makes a comeback	*Jazz*, a ten-part documentary by much acclaimed filmmaker Ken Burns, is shown worldwide

1960s   1970s   1980s   1990s

Instruments of Jazz Music

Jazz bands tend to have a wider range of instruments than rock bands. The most popular instruments used in jazz are the trumpet, clarinet, saxophone, drums, piano, and electronic keyboard.

Trumpet

The trumpet is a brass instrument with three valves that regulate the amount of sound that travels through the instrument's tubing. This determines the pitch of the sound produced. As the trumpet can make a very loud sound, it is often fitted with a mute. This is a cone-shaped object that reduces the volume. The sharp, brassy sound of the trumpet stands out from other instruments and it features strongly in the history of jazz. Among the great trumpet players are Louis Armstrong, Bix Beiderbecke, and Dizzy Gillespie.

Trumpet, fitted with a mute

Saxophone

The saxophone is a **reed instrument**. There are four types of saxophone: the soprano, alto, tenor, and baritone. Like the human voice, the soprano has the highest pitch, alto is the next pitch down, then tenor, then baritone. The most popular saxophone is the tenor, then the alto. The saxophone is the only instrument that is used more in jazz than in any other form of music. Charlie "Bird" Parker is considered the greatest jazz saxophonist.

Tenor saxophone

Alto saxophone

Soprano saxophone

Clarinet

Clarinet

The clarinet is a reed instrument that has a gentler sound than the trumpet. The clarinet reached its peak in popularity during the 1930s and 1940s, when it was played by swing band leaders such as Benny Goodman and Artie Shaw.

Drums

Drums are an essential part of a jazz band. They keep every musician in time. One main difference between jazz drummers and rock and pop drummers is that jazz players often use special wire brushes rather than drumsticks to produce a slightly tinny sound on the snare drum and cymbals. The most famous jazz drummer was Gene Krupa, who led his own band.

Piano

The piano has always played a major role in jazz music. Early jazz pianists, particularly Fats Waller, developed the jazz piano style known as "stride," in which the pianist keeps time with the left hand and uses the right hand to play the melody and to improvize. Many modern jazz performers have incorporated electronic keyboards in their music. Other than Fats Waller, the greatest jazz pianists include Count Basie, Dave Brubeck, and Duke Ellington.

A drum kit. The bass drum is the large drum at the front. It is pedal-operated by a **mallet**. The snare drum is the narrow-sided drum on the right at the back. The toms are the two smaller drums suspended above the bass drum, and a floor tom is on the far left. The instruments that look like large plates are the cymbals: ride cymbal (left); crash cymbal (highest on right); and high hat (below, right), which is pedal-operated.

Jazz Musicians and Less Common Instruments

Stephane Grappelli (1908–1997): violin
Red Norvo (1908–1999): xylophone
Django Reinhart (1910–1953): acoustic guitar
Adele Girard (1913–1993): harp
Yusef Lateef (born in 1920): flute
Don Cherry (1936–1995): gong, bamboo flute, and horns made from bone
Rahsaan Roland Kirk (1936–1977): whistles and manzello
Herbie Hancock (born in 1940): synthesiser
Gary Burton (born in 1943): vibraphone
Michael Brecker (born in 1949): electronic wind instruments

An upright piano

Great Jazz Performers

Other Great Jazz Horn and Reed Players

King Oliver (1885–1938): cornet
Sidney Bechet (1897–1959): clarinet
Bix Beiderbecke (1903–1931): cornet
Jimmy Dorsey (1904–1957): clarinet
Glenn Miller (1904–1944): trombone
Tommy Dorsey (1905–1956): trombone
Jack Teagarden (1905–1964): trombone
Woody Herman (1913–1987): clarinet
Dizzy Gillespie (1917–1993): trumpet
Charlie "Bird" Parker (1920–1955): saxophone
John Coltrane (1926–1967): saxophone
Stan Getz (1927–1991): saxophone
Chet Baker (1929–1988): trumpet
Acker Bilk (born in 1929): clarinet
Artie Shaw (1944–1989): clarinet
James Morrison (born in 1962): trumpet

Most jazz performers are strongly identified with the instruments that they play. The greatest jazz musicians not only play an instrument but also lead their own band. Some musicians sing and play, while other performers only sing.

Louis Armstrong

Born August 4, 1901, New Orleans, Louisiana, United States (died 1971)
Full name Louis Armstrong
Instruments/roles trumpet, **vocals**, composer, bandleader
Style New Orleans
Hit songs include "Heebie Jeebies" (1926), "When the Saints Go Marching In" (1938), "Hello Dolly" (1963), "What a Wonderful World" (1967)
Profile Armstrong learned the trumpet while in a boys' home. He started his professional career as second trumpet in King Oliver's Band but was soon recognized as the greatest jazz trumpet player in the music industry. He was nicknamed "Satchmo," which was short for "Satchelmouth." Armstrong was one of the few jazz musicians to have No. 1 hits in the music charts after rock music came on the scene in the late 1950s.

Louis Armstrong

Benny Goodman

Born May 30, 1909, Chicago, Illinois, United States (died 1986)
Full name Benjamin David Goodman
Instruments/roles clarinet, saxophone, composer, bandleader
Style swing
Hit songs include "Moon Glow" (1934), "It's Been so Long" (1936), "Sing, Sing, Sing" (1937), "Don't Be That Way" (1938)
Profile Goodman made his first professional appearance in 1921 and his first solo recording in 1926. One of the earliest non-African Americans to become a jazz star, he was one of those responsible for making jazz popular with non-African Americans.

Miles Davis

Born May 26, 1926, Alton, Illinois, United States (died 1991)
Full name Miles Dewey Davis
Instruments/roles trumpet, flugelhorn, composer, bandleader
Styles cool jazz, be-bop
Hit songs include "Walkin" (1954), "Solar" (1954), "So What" (1959)
Profile Considered the father of modern jazz, Davis was forever trying new things. He came from a musical family and began playing the trumpet when he was 13 years old. Within two years, he was playing professionally. In 1955, the five members of the Miles Davis Quintet, which included legendary saxophonist John Coltrane, recorded six albums in just 12 months.

Wynton Marsalis

Born October 18, 1961, New Orleans, Louisiana, United States
Full name Wynton Marsalis
Instruments/roles trumpet, composer
Styles be-bop (also classical music)
Hit songs include "Delfeayo's Dilemma" (1985), "J Mood" (1986), "Blue Interlude" (1992)
Profile Marsalis comes from a family rich in jazz traditions. His father is a pianist and composer, one of his brothers is a drummer, another a saxophonist, and a third a trombonist. Marsalis combines jazz and classical music more successfully and more regularly than any other musician.

Miles Davis

More Great Jazz Performers

Duke Ellington

 Other Great Jazz Pianists

"Jelly Roll" Morton (1890–1941)

Earl "Fatha" Hines (1903–1983)

Fats Waller (1904–1943)

Art Tatum (1909–1956)

Thelonious Monk (1917–1982)

Dave Brubeck (born in 1920)

Oscar Peterson (born in 1925)

Duke Ellington

Born April 29, 1899, Washington DC,
United States (died 1974)
Full name Edward Kennedy Ellington
Instruments/roles piano, composer, bandleader
Styles be-bop, swing
Hit songs include "Mood Indigo" (1931),
"It Don't Mean a Thing If it Ain't Got That
Swing" (1932), "Sophisticated Lady" (1933)
Profile Ellington began playing piano from the
age of seven and developed an interest in jazz
at a very early age. In his music he combined
many forms of jazz, and this has been
responsible for his ongoing success.

Count Basie

Born August 21, 1904, Red Bank, New Jersey,
United States (died 1984)
Full name William Basie
Instruments/roles piano, organ, composer,
bandleader
Style swing
Hit songs include "One O'Clock Jump" (1937),
"Doggin' Around" (1938), "April in Paris"
(1955), "Everyday I Have the Blues" (1955)
Profile Basie played with several bands in his
late teens and early twenties. In 1927 he was
stranded in Kansas City, which was one of
the main centers of jazz in the United States.
Here he gained experience with many great
musicians and his career took off. He toured the
world many times, spreading jazz far and wide.

Billie Holiday

Born April 7, 1915, Baltimore, Maryland, United States (died 1959)
Full name Eleanor Holiday
Instruments/roles vocals
Styles be-bop, swing (also blues)
Hit songs include "Strange Fruit" (1939), "God Bless the Child" (1941), "Solitude" (1941), "Lover Man" (1941)
Profile Holiday lived a tragic, violent life that was reflected in her emotional, soulful voice. She worked with some of the great jazz composers and musicians including Count Basie, Artie Shaw, and Louis Armstrong. Sadly, she died from a drug overdose. Her recordings are still among the top-selling jazz albums each year.

Billie Holiday

Ella Fitzgerald

Born April 25, 1918, Newport, Virginia, United States (died 1996)
Full name Ella Fitzgerald
Instruments/roles vocals, composer, bandleader
Styles be-bop, swing, New Orleans
Hit songs include "A-tisket, A-tasket" (1938), "Undecided" (1939), "Jersey Bounce" (1961)
Profile Fitzgerald was the most influential woman in jazz. She began her professional career after winning an amateur talent quest in 1934, went on to work with Chick Webb's band, then became a bandleader herself. She often appeared and recorded with Louis Armstrong. She is particularly well known for her **scat** singing, a style in which the performer sings nonsense sounds.

Other Great Jazz Vocalists

"Ma" Rainey (1886–1939)
Cab Calloway (1907–1994)
Sarah Vaughan (1924–1990)
Cleo Laine (born in 1927)
Nina Simone (1933–2003)

Cleo Laine

Great Jazz Compositions

A jazz composition does not have to feature vocals to be a hit. Many jazz classics are instrumentals.

"Black and Tan Fantasy"

Year released 1927
Writers Duke Ellington and Bubber Miley
Performers Duke Ellington and his Orchestra
This tune was the first of many Ellington classics and the one that made him popular with non-African American audiences.

"Heebie Jeebies"

Year released 1926
Writer Boyd Atkins
Performers Louis Armstrong and his Hot Five
This was Armstrong's first big hit and the first to feature the scat style of singing.

The Grammy Hall of Fame

More than 60 jazz "recordings–singles" have been inducted into the **Grammy** Hall of Fame since it was established in 1973. Songs can only gain admission to the Grammy Hall of Fame 25 years after their first release. The first date is the year of **induction**. The second date is the year of the song's release by the named performer or group.

1974	**"Body and Soul"** (1939) Coleman Hawkins
	"West End Blues" (1928) Louis Armstrong and his Hot Five
1975	**"Mood Indigo"** (1931) Duke Ellington
1976	**"God Bless the Child"** (1941) Billie Holiday
	"Take the 'A' Train" (1941) Duke Ellington and his Orchestra
1977	**"Begin the Beguine"** (1939) Artie Shaw and his Orchestra
	"Singin' the Blues" (1927) Frankie Trumbauer and his Orchestra with Bix Beiderbecke
1978	**"Strange Fruit"** (1939) Billie Holiday
1979	**"One O'Clock Jump"** (1937) Count Basie and his Barons of Rhythm

Benny Goodman, on clarinet, and Stan Getz, on saxophone, were two of the great stars of the jazz era.

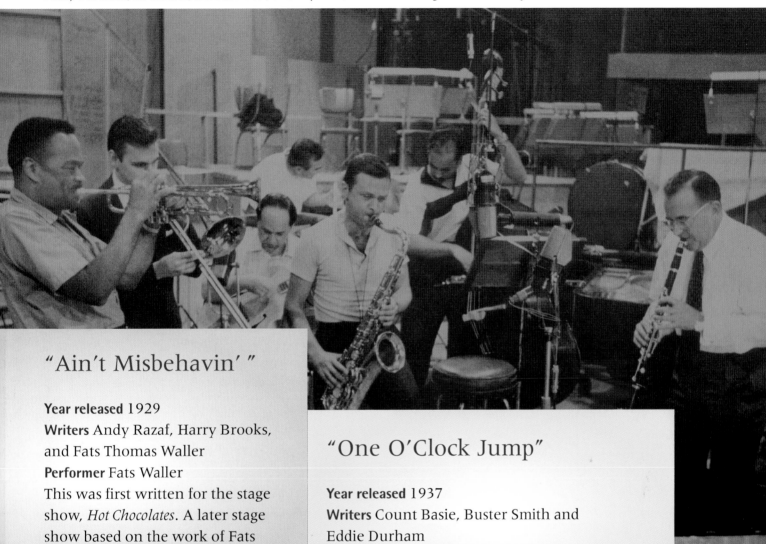

"Ain't Misbehavin' "

Year released 1929
Writers Andy Razaf, Harry Brooks, and Fats Thomas Waller
Performer Fats Waller
This was first written for the stage show, *Hot Chocolates*. A later stage show based on the work of Fats Waller was named after this song and won a Tony Award for Best Musical.

"One O'Clock Jump"

Year released 1937
Writers Count Basie, Buster Smith and Eddie Durham
Performers Count Basie and his Barons of Rhythm
This was the first of many Count Basie songs to hit the charts and is typical of the "Basie sound."

1980	**"In a Mist"** (1927) Bix Beiderbecke	1986	**"Tea for Two"** (1939) Art Tatum
1981	**"Black and Tan Fantasy"** (1927) Duke Ellington and his Orchestra	1987	**"And the Angels Sing"** (1939) Benny Goodman and his Orchestra
1982	**"Sing, Sing, Sing"** (1937) Benny Goodman and his Orchestra	1988	**"Star Dust"** (1940) Artie Shaw and his Orchestra
1983	**"Pine Top's Boogie Woogie"** (1928) Pine Top Smith	1989	**"Lover Man"** (1945) Billie Holiday
1984	**"Ain't Misbehavin' "** (1929) Fats Waller		**"Ornithology"** (1946) Charlie Parker Sextet
	"Four Brothers" (1948) Woody Herman and his Orchestra	1990	**"Black, Brown and Beige"** (1944) Duke Ellington and his Orchestra
1985	**"April in Paris"** (1955) Count Basie Orchestra		
	"Artistry in Rhythm" (1945) Stan Kenton and his Orchestra	1991	**"Misty"** (1954) Erroll Garner Trio
1986	**"A-tisket, A-tasket"** (1938) Chick Webb and his Orchestra with Ella Fitzgerald	1992	**"Everyday (I Have the Blues)"** (1955) Count Basie Orchestra
		1993	**"Round About Midnight"** (1948) Thelonious Monk Quintet

More Great Jazz Compositions

Ella Fitzgerald

"A-tisket, A-tasket"

Year released 1938
Writers Ella Fitzgerald and Van Alexander (based on a traditional nursery rhyme)
Performers Chick Webb and his Orchestra with Ella Fitzgerald
Featuring Fizgerald's scat style of singing, this song went to No. 1 on the music charts. It boosted the popularity of Chick Webb and his Orchestra and launched Ella Fitzgerald on the road to stardom.

"Sing, Sing, Sing"

Year released 1937
Writer Louis Prima
Performers Benny Goodman and his Orchestra
The moment Benny Goodman and his Orchestra played this song live at New York's Carnegie Hall in January 1938, swing music took off. While most jazz hits are reasonably short tunes, "Sing, Sing, Sing" goes for 15 minutes.

BELOW The recordings–singles that were inducted into the Grammy Hall of Fame between 1993 and 2002.

1993	"St. Louis Blues" (1925) Bessie Smith and Louis Armstrong	1998	"Moonglow" (1936) Benny Goodman Quartet
1994	"Crazy Blues" (1920) Ma Smith and her Jazz Hounds		"Straighten up and Fly Right" (1944) King Cole Trio
1996	"Chimes Blues" (1923) King Oliver's Creole Jazz Band	1999	"Diminuendo and Crescendo in Blue" (1956) Duke Ellington and his Orchestra
	"Flying Home" (1942) Lionel Hampton and his Orchestra		"Djangology" (1935) Django Reinhardt and Stephane Grappelli
	"Take Five" (1959) Dave Brubeck Quartet		"For Dancers Only" (1937) Jimmie Lunceford and his Orchestra
1997	"Mack the Knife" (1955) Louis Armstrong and the All-Stars		"Heebie Jeebies" (1926) Louis Armstrong and his Hot Five
1998	"Cherokee" (1939) Charlie Barnet and his Orchestra		"Honeysuckle Rose" (1934) Fats Waller
	"If You Could See Me Now" (1946) Sarah Vaughan		"Just You, Just Me" (1944) Lester Young Quartet
	"Moanin' " (1958) Art Blakey and the Jazz Messengers		

"Take Five"

Year released 1959
Writer Paul Desmond
Performers Dave Brubeck Quartet
The first jazz instrumental to sell over a million copies, this is the best known piece of jazz music. It won many new fans to jazz, with rock musician Billy Joel even claiming that it was one of the most important pieces of music he had heard.

"Hello Dolly"

Year released 1963
Writer Jerry Herman
Performer Louis Armstrong
This was the title song of a film of the same name and in which Armstrong appeared. The song became a huge hit for Armstrong, almost 50 years after his first hit, which is a measure of his greatness. "Hello Dolly" has since been recorded by many other artists, but not with the success of Armstrong.

Jill Perryman starred in a production of the 1990s musical, *Hello Dolly*.

1999	**"Manteca"** (1947) Dizzy Gillespie and his Orchestra
	"Minnie the Moocher" (1931) Cab Calloway and his Orchestra
	"Now He Sings, Now He Sobs" (1968) Chick Corea
	"Un Poco Loco" (1951) Bud Powell Trio
2000	**"Desafinado"** (1962) Stan Getz and Charlie Byrd
	"Early Autumn" (1949) Woody Herman and his Orchestra
	"Frenesi" (1940) Artie Shaw and his Orchestra
	"Groovin' High" (1945) Dizzy Gillespie and his Sextet
2000	**"I Loves You, Porgy"** (1959) Nina Simone
	"Lush Life" (1963) John Coltrane with Johnny Hartman
	"Nuages" (1946) Django Reinhardt and Stephane Grappelli
2001	**"Moody's Mood For Love"** (1952) James Moody
2002	**"(Get Your Kicks On) Route 66"** (1946) The King Cole Trio
	"Billie's Bounce" (1945) Charlie Parker and his Re-Boppers
	"How High the Moon" (1960) Ella Fitzgerald
	"Woodchopper's Ball" (1939) Woody Herman and his Orchestra

Blues Music

Blues music is a type of African-American folk music. It is related to jazz, but separate from it. Blues got its name because it expressed the emotions of sadness, hardship, and love gone wrong. The vocal style developed from southern work songs and, like jazz, the music relies heavily on improvization.

Structure of Blues Music

Blues songs generally follow a standard format, known as a 12-**bar** structure. Each verse consists of three lines and each line is made up of four bars, making a total of 12 bars.

Unlike jazz, blues does not need a lot of musicians and many of its best songs consist of just vocals and a guitar.

Playing the Blues

The main aim of a blues song is not to tell a story but to express the emotions of the singer, and these are generally sad or tragic. The lyrics deal with basic human problems, such as love, poverty, and death.

However, the main idea of performing blues music is to make audiences feel better about themselves. The words and music in blues songs suggest unhappiness but, if you listen carefully, they often tell listeners to take control of their lives and work to make things better.

One of the legends of blues, 73-year-old Ray Charles, still performs regularly at international blues festivals.

Twelve-bar Structure

Blues songs are full of words and music that are repeated. The verses are divided into three sections, each four bars long—making a total of 12 bars in each verse. In the first four bars, a singer will express his or her emotions. Then the words are repeated in the next four bars (with slight variations) and, finally, the singer will produce a response to the first two lines. Here is an example:

I am waiting, waiting, waiting for my gal.
Yeah, I am waiting, waiting, waiting for my gal.
But I know, she ain't never coming back to me.

The lyrics are very sad, describing a man waiting for his woman, who he knows will not return. However, because blues songs are supposed to make one feel better, the last verse of the song might go like this:

I'm sick of waiting, waiting, waiting for my gal.
Yeah, I'm sick of waiting, waiting, waiting for my gal.
So I'll just go and find myself someone new.

Rhythm and Blues

The blues are sometimes confused with rhythm and blues, or R&B. This was a popular music style performed mainly by African-Americans from the late 1940s to the early 1960s. It grew out of blues music but is played by a group, usually a lead singer, a rhythm section (bass, drums, piano, and guitar), and voices.

Many rock musicians, particularly the Rolling Stones and Eric Clapton, claim that rhythm and blues was the major influence on their music.

History of Blues Music

Non-musicians Inducted in the Blues Hall of Fame

1994 **John Richbourg, Gene Nobles and Bill "Hoss" Allen** (disc jockeys from WLAC Nashville)

John and Alan Lomax (recorders of traditional blues music)

1995 **Leonard and Phil Chess** (founders of Chess Records)

1996 **Pete Welding** (founder of Testament Records)

Bob Koester (founder of Delmark Records)

1997 **Bruce Iglauer** (founder of Alligator Records)

1998 **Sam Phillips** (founder of Sun Records)

Lillian Shedd McMurry (founder of Trumpet Records)

1999 **Chris Strachwitz** (founder of Arhoolie Records)

Lester Melrose (record producer)

2000 **Dick Waterman** (photographer)

2001 **Robert Palmer** (writer)

Theresa Needham (promoter)

2002 **Jim O'Neal** (writer and publisher)

Like jazz, blues started among the plantation slaves in the southern United States. It was based on a form of communication called "call and response," which was a feature of African music. It involved one singer calling out, or "hollering," and another returning the call with their own "holler." This became known as the "field holler," or "field shout."

The 1800s

After slavery ended in 1863, African-Americans had more freedom of expression. By the end of the 1800s, blues music, born out of the cruel experiences of slave labor, was well established in African-American communities in the southern United States.

Early 1900s

The popularity of the blues increased, but blues songs were not recorded or published. Generally they were not even written down. This is because the early blues musicians were playing for passion rather than money. Thousands of blues songs have since been recorded, but thousands more have disappeared because they were only performed in front of a live audience, in clubs or simply on the streets.

The timeline gives important blues events from the 1890s to the 1990s.

1890s	1912	1917	1920	1923	1925	1933
The field holler develops into a music style called blues	W. C. Handy's "Memphis Blues" is the first blues song to be published	Blues legend Lead Belly is sent to prison for murder	Ma Smith's "Crazy Blues" is the first vocal blues song to be recorded	Bessie Smith's "Down-hearted Blues" sells over 750,000 copies and makes her the first blues superstar	Lead Belly is set free from prison after writing and performing a song pleading for his release	Robert Johnson is encouraged by leading blues guitarists to start playing the blues

1890s   1900s   1910s   1920s   1930s

Blues Music Becomes Known

In 1912, W. C. Handy's "Memphis Blues" was the first blues song to be published. By the time World War I broke out in 1914, the blues was established as a serious form of music. During the war, soldiers from the southern states sang the blues songs on the battlefields. By the end of the war in 1918, all the American soldiers recognized the blues and the music grew in popularity on their return home.

The 1920s

Throughout the 1920s, blues musicians still mainly lived and worked in the southern states. However, in 1929, the United States was hit by the Great Depression. It was a time in which jobs were hard to find and many people struggled to feed their families. Many African-Americans from the south, including blues musicians, moved north in search of work. The blues were about to spread far and wide.

After the Depression

The blues musicians established themselves in the big northern cities of the United States and began playing to larger audiences. Many were given recording contracts. When the electric guitar was introduced in the 1940s, many blues musicians swapped their **acoustic** guitars for the louder versions.

When rock music arrived on the scene in the mid-1950s, many of the young rock stars claimed to have been heavily influenced by some of the great legends of blues. These included Muddy Waters, John Lee Hooker, T-Bone Walker, and B. B. King. King went on to incorporate elements of rock music in his blues.

Two **inductees** of the Blues Hall of Fame, guitarist Brownie McGhee and harp player Sonny Terry. These two players formed one of the longest-lasting duos in blues history.

1948	1958	1962	1970	1992
Muddy Waters moves to Chicago where his blues playing enchants a wide audience	W. C. Handy, the "father of blues," dies and a film about his life stars Nat King Cole as Handy	Jazz great Oscar Peterson records an album, *Night Train*, that pays tribute to the blues	B. B. King records "The Thrill is Gone," successfully combining blues and rock music	John Lee Hooker is inducted into the Rock and Roll Hall of Fame
John Lee Hooker records "Boogie Chillen" and puts the blues into the music charts				

| 1940s | 1950s | 1960s | 1970s | 1980s | 1990s |

Instruments of Blues Music

In the early 1900s, the blues was usually played by a single guitarist. As its popularity grew, musicians got together to record songs but they did not always form bands. Today, blues bands often feature a star performer out front with a low-profile backing group.

Guitar

The guitar is the central instrument in blues music. Early blues singers sometimes had a harmonica player and pianist to back them but generally they performed alone, carrying their guitar around from club to club and town to town. Since the 1940s, many blues guitarists have used an electric guitar. However, some traditional blues guitarists believe that blues should only be played with an acoustic guitar.

Banjo

The banjo is a five-string instrument that originated in Africa. It gained popularity in the southern United States in the mid-1800s, when African-Americans used it to play **minstrel music**. The banjo was the main string instrument in the early days of the blues, before the guitar became widely adopted.

Six-string acoustic guitar

Twelve-string acoustic guitar

Banjo

Harmonica

The harmonica is also known as the mouth organ. Its sound is a great **accompaniment** to the mournful emotions that are expressed in blues songs.

The harmonica was invented in the early 1800s by a German named Christian Buschmann. It was based on the keys of an organ and consists of a number of reeds placed inside a metal box, with small openings along the edge. The instrument is played by moving it along the mouth and blowing air into, or sucking air out of, the openings.

Blues musicians call the harmonica the "blues harp." Some play the guitar and the harmonica at the same time by attaching the harmonica to a frame that fits around their neck. Their hands are then free to play the guitar. The great harmonica players include Big Walter Horton, Howlin' Wolf, Junior Wells, George "Harmonica" Smith, Sonny Boy Williamson I, and Sonny Boy Williamson II.

Harmonica

Fiddle

When a blues musician is accompanied by a band, one of the other musicians is usually a fiddle player. A fiddle is a violin. One of the great blues fiddle players was Butch Cage, who played for more than 40 years alongside guitarist Willie Thomas.

Fiddle and bow

Washboard

Mandolin

Accordion

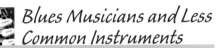

Blues Musicians and Less Common Instruments

Lynn August (born in 1948): accordion

Juke Boy Bonner (1932–1978): one-man band

Johnny Dodds (1892–1940): clarinet

Simmie Dooley (1881–1961): kazoo

Uaroy Graves (dates unknown): tambourine

Johnny Heartsman (born in 1937): organ

Andy Kulberg (born in 1944): flute

Hot Lips Page (1908–1954): trumpet

Sam Washboard (1910–1966): washboard

Johnny Young (1918–1974): mandolin

Great Blues Performers

Most of the great blues musicians have been African-Americans. An explanation for this was offered by one of the great blues legends, Lead Belly. He claimed that only African-Americans sang the blues because "no white man ever had the blues, 'cause [they had] nothing to worry about."

W. C. Handy

Born November 16, 1873, Florence, Alabama, United States (died 1958)
Full name William Christopher Handy
Hit songs include "Memphis Blues" (1912), "St. Louis Blues" (1914), "Beale Street Blues" (1916), "Joe Turner Blues" (1915)
Profile Handy referred to himself as "the father of the blues." Unlike many early blues performers, he was a trained musician. Throughout his career, he often complained that blues was too simple and monotonous to play, yet he could never get it out of his system. He contributed to the blues as a musician, publisher, and songwriter. The Blues Foundation Awards are named after him.

Lead Belly

Born January 21, 1888, Shiloh, Louisiana, United States (died 1949)
Full name Huddie Ledbetter
Hit songs include "Angola Blues" (1933), "Midnight Special" (1934), "Rock Island Line" (1937), "Goodnight Irene" (1941)
Profile One of the most colorful figures in blues music, Lead Belly was "discovered" while serving time in jail for attempted murder. It was his second jail sentence, and he seemed set to spend the rest of his life strumming his guitar behind bars. However, **musicologist** Alan Lomax visited the jail and was amazed by what he heard. Lomax convinced the authorities to release Lead Belly, so that he could record and perform his music.

The Blues Hall of Fame

The Blues Hall of Fame recognizes the great achievements of those involved in blues music. There have been 80 performers inducted into the Blues Hall of Fame since it was established in 1980. The first date is the year of induction.

1980	Howlin' Wolf (1910–1976)	1980	Lightnin' Hopkins (1912–1982)
	Bobby "Blue" Bland (born in 1930)		John Lee Hooker (1920–2001)
	Little Walter (1930–1968)		Willie Dixon (1915–1992)
	B. B. King (born in 1925)		Roy Brown (1925–1981)
	Robert Johnson (1911–1938)		Big Bill Broonzy (1893–1958)
	Elmore James (1918–1963)		Blind Lemon Jefferson (1897–1929)
	Son House (1902–1988)	1981	Jimmy Reed (1925–1976)

Bessie Smith

Bessie Smith

Born April 15, 1894, Chattanooga, Tennessee, United States (died 1937)

Full name Bessie Smith

Hit songs include "Gulf Coast Blues" (1923), "Down Hearted Blues" (1923), "Nobody Knows You When You're Down and Out" (1929)

Profile Bessie Smith was largely responsible for widening the appeal of the blues in the early 1900s. She was the first blues recording star. She also managed to take control of her career in a way that most other blues and jazz women could not. Known as the "Queen of Blues," she was asked to sing with many of the leading jazz performers, including Louis Armstrong. Even today, her recordings are among the best-selling blues albums/CDs.

1981   Bessie Smith (1894–1937)
        Sonny Boy Williamson I (1914–1948)
        Sonny Boy Williamson II (1910–1965)
        Tampa Red (1904–1981)
        Professor Longhair (1918–1980)
        Charley Patton (1891–1934)
        Muddy Waters (1915–1983)

1981   Memphis Minnie (1897–1973)
        Blind Willie McTell (1901–1959)
        Otis Spann (1930–1970)
1982   Freddie King (1934–1976)
        Magic Sam (1937–1969)
        Big Walter Horton (1917–1981)
        Ray Charles (born in 1930)
        Leroy Carr (1905–1935)

1983   Albert King (1923–1992)
        Robert Nighthawk (1909–1967)
        "Ma" Rainey (1886–1939)
        Big Joe Turner (1911–1985)
        Louis Jordan (1908–1975)
1984   Otis Rush (born in 1934)
        Hound Dog Taylor (1917–1975)
        Big Mama Thornton (1926–1984)

More Great Blues Performers

Blind Lemon Jefferson

Blind Lemon Jefferson

Born July 1897, Couchman, Texas, United States (died 1929)
Full name Clarence Jefferson
Hit songs include "Long Lonesome Blues" (1926), "Jack O'Diamonds" (1926), "Match Box Blues" (1927), "See That My Grave is Kept Clean" (1928)
Profile Jefferson's recording career lasted only three years, from 1926 to 1929, but he recorded over 100 songs. As well as his own hits, Jefferson wrote hit songs for other blues artists. Many of the successful blues musicians who followed Jefferson claimed him as a major influence in their career. Bob Dylan recorded a version of the 1928 song in 1962.

Robert Johnson

Born May 8, 1911, Hazelhurst, Mississippi, United States (died 1938)
Full name Robert Johnson
Hit songs include "I Believe I'll Dust My Broom" (1936), "Sweet Home Chicago" (1936), "Walkin' Blues" (1936), "Me and the Devil Blues" (1937)
Profile Johnson was a singer, guitarist, and composer. He was one of the biggest influences in blues music even though he died at the age of 27 and only had two recording sessions. He was a true blues musician, traveling the southern states playing his songs. Along the way, he was influenced by others, and left behind young blues musicians overwhelmed by what they had heard.

The list below names the inductees to the Blues Hall of Fame, 1985–2003.

1985	J. B. Hutto (1926–1983)	1987	Eddie Taylor (1923–1985)	1990	Bukka White (1909–1977)
	Slim Harpo (1924–1970)		Sonny Terry (1911–1986)		Blind Blake (early 1890s–1933)
	Chuck Berry (born in 1926)	1988	Little Milton (born in 1934)		Jay McShann (born in 1916)
	Buddy Guy (born in 1936)		Johnny Winter (born in 1944)		Mississippi John Hurt (1893–1966)
1986	Tommy Johnson (1896–1956)	1989	Memphis Slim (1915–1988)	1991	Sleepy John Estes (1904–1977)
	Lead Belly (1888–1949)		Clifton Chenier (1925–1987)		Fred McDowell (1904–1972)
	Albert Collins (1932–1993)		Robert Jr Lockwood (born in 1915)	1992	Big Joe Williams (1903–1982)
1987	Percy Mayfield (1920–1984)	1990	Lonnie Johnson (1894–1970)		Johnny Shines (1915–1992)

Muddy Waters

Born April 4, 1915, Rolling Fork, Mississippi, United States (died 1983)
Full name McKinley Morganfield
Hit songs include "Rollin' Stone" (1950), "I'm Your Hoochie Coochie Man" (1953),
"Baby, Please Don't Go" (1953), "Got My Mojo Working" (1957)
Profile Muddy Waters, like some other famous blues artists, was discovered by musicologist Alan Lomax, who encouraged him to make his first recordings. Muddy moved to Chicago in the early 1940s and was responsible for shaping the blues sound in that city. He formed a blues band, which toured America and overseas. He has been an inspiration to countless blues and rock musicians. He was always open to other forms of music, including folk and rock, and in the late 1960s he recorded a psychedelic album called *Electric Mud*.

B. B. King

Born September 16, 1925, Indianola, Mississippi, United States
Full name Riley B. King
Hit songs include "Three O'Clock Blues" (1951), "You Know I Love You" (1952), "Everyday I Have the Blues" (1955), "The Thrill Is Gone" (1970)
Profile When he was in his twenties, B. B. King moved to Memphis, Tennessee, where his career took off. No other blues musician has done so much to give blues a wider audience. He incorporated rock in his blues music, and became a major influence on rock stars Eric Clapton, Jeff Beck, and Jimmy Page. King is the best-selling blues musician of all time.

B. B. King

1992	**Skip James** (1902–1969)	1996	**David "Honeyboy" Edwards** (born in 1915)	1999	**Roosevelt Sykes** (1906–1984)
1993	**Champion Jack Dupree** (1909–1992)	1997	**Koko Taylor** (born in 1935)	2000	**Stevie Ray Vaughan** (1954–1990)
	Lowell Fulson (1921–1999)		**Brownie McGhee** (1915–1996)		**Johnny Otis** (born in 1921)
1994	**Arthur "Big Boy" Crudup** (1905–1974)	1998	**Junior Wells** (1934–1998)	2001	**Etta James** (born in 1938)
			Luther Allison (1939–1997)		**Little Junior Parker** (1932–1971)
1995	**Jimmy Rogers** (1924–1997)	1999	**Clarence "Gatemouth" Brown** (born in 1924)		**Rufus Thomas** (1917–2001)
1996	**Charles Brown** (1922–1999)			2002	**Big Maceo** (1905–1953)

Great Blues Compositions

Blues songs, traditionally, were sad songs that grew out of the experience of slavery in America's deep south. Blues music is unique in that all true blues songs have one common theme, which is the blues.

"Memphis Blues"

Year released 1912
Writer W. C. Handy
Performer W. C. Handy
First called "Mr Crump" (1908), this was written to help the re-election chances of the mayor of Memphis, E. H. "Boss" Crump. Handy changed the words and title in 1912 and it became a huge hit.

"I'm Your Hoochie Coochie Man"

Year released 1953
Writer Willie Dixon
Performer Muddy Waters
This song combines the talents of three of the most influential figures in blues, including the harmonica playing of Little Walter, one of the greatest blues harp players.

"See That My Grave is Kept Clean"

Year released 1928
Writer Blind Lemon Jefferson
Performer Blind Lemon Jefferson
Recorded a year before Jefferson's death, the words in the title are engraved on his tombstone.

"I Believe I'll Dust My Broom"

Year released 1936
Writer Robert Johnson
Performer Robert Johnson
Also recorded by Muddy Waters and B. B. King, this is one of the most recorded blues songs.

The Blues Hall of Fame

There have been 37 recordings inducted into the Blues Hall of Fame. Some of them are listed here.

1981 **"Sweet Home Chicago"** (1936)
Robert Johnson
1982 **"I'm Your Hoochie Coochie Man"** (1953)
Muddy Waters
1983 **"Dust My Broom"** (1951) Elmore James

1985 **"Boogie Chillen"** (1948) John Lee Hooker
"Smoke Stack Lightning" (1968)
Howlin' Wolf
"The Thrill is Gone" (1951) B. B. King
1986 **"Cross Road Blues"** (1936)
Robert Johnson
1987 **"Manish Boy"** (1955) Muddy Waters
1988 **"Come On In My Kitchen"** (1936)
Robert Johnson
1990 **"Terraplane Blues"** (1936) Robert Johnson
1991 **"The Killing Floor"** (1964) Howlin' Wolf

1992 **"Baby Please Don't Go"** (1935)
Big Joe Williams
1994 **"I Can't Quit You Baby"** (1956) Otis Rush
1996 **"Don't Start Me Talkin'"** (1955)
Sonny Boy Williamson II
1998 **"Messin' With The Kid"** (1960) Jnr Wells
2000 **"Down Home Blues"** (1982) ZZ Hill
2001 **"Shake, Rattle and Roll"** (1954)
Big Joe Turner
2002 **"Goin' Down Slow"** (1941)
St Louis Jimmy Oden

Glossary

accompaniment   support or backing provided by instruments (or voices)

acoustic   having a sound made naturally, rather than made louder by electronic means

bar   vertical line drawn across the stave in a piece of written music, to separate groups of notes; also refers to the group of notes between two bars

bass   the lowest part in a piece of music (for an instrument) and the lowest pitch for a male voice

commercial   appealing to a wide audience, or profitable

experimentation   trying something new or different

Grammy   the major music award in the United States

improvization   making up on the spot or without preparation

improvize   to make up on the spot

inductees   people elected to join a group, such as the Hall of Fame

induction   election or introduction

instrumentals   music featuring instruments but no voices

lyrics   words to a song

mallet   hammer-like tool with a head made of rubber, metal, or wood

minstrel music   popular musical entertainment made up of song and dance, first performed by whites impersonating blacks, but later performed by African-Americans only

musicologist   someone who studies music

reed instrument   instrument with a mouthpiece made of cane or metal, which vibrates when blown into (in some instruments, such as the accordion and concertina, the reed is operated by air blown from a bellows)

revivals   repeats

scat   singing style that involves singing nonsense syllables

score   written copy of a piece of music

solo   one single performer, or instrument, playing on its own

syncopation   putting an emphasis on musical beats that are normally in the background

vocals   the singing part of a song

Index

B

be-bop 8, 9, 13, 14, 15
blues compositions 30
    "I Believe I'll Dust My Broom"
       28, 30
    "I'm Your Hoochie Coochie
       Man" 29, 30
    "Memphis Blues" 22, 23, 26,
       30
    "See That My Grave is Kept
       Clean" 28, 30
    "The Thrill is Gone" 23, 29, 30
Blues Hall of Fame 22, 23, 26–9,
    30
blues performers 26–9
    Cage, Butch 25
    Charles, Ray 21, 27
    Handy, W. C 22, 23, 26, 30
    Hooker, John Lee 23, 26, 30
    Horton, Big Walter 25, 27
    Jefferson, Blind Lemon 26,
       28, 30
    Johnson, Robert 22, 26, 28,
       30
    King, B. B 23, 26, 29, 30
    Lead Belly 22, 26, 28
    McGhee, Brownie 23, 29
    Smith, Bessie 18, 22, 27
    Smith, George "Harmonica"
       25
    Terry, Sonny 23, 28
    Thomas, Willie 25
    Walker, T-Bone 23
    Walter, Little 26, 30
    Waters, Muddy 23, 27, 29, 30
    Wells, Junior 25, 29, 30
    Williamson I, Sonny Boy 25,
       27
    Williamson II, Sonny Boy 25,
       27, 30
    Wolf, Howlin' 25, 26, 30
blues timeline 22–3
boogie woogie 7
bossa nova 9

C

Chicago style jazz 7
cool jazz 9, 13

F

free jazz 9
fusion 9

G

Grammy Hall of Fame 16–19

H

hot jazz 7

I

improvization 5, 6, 8, 9, 20
instruments
    blues 24–5
    jazz 10–11

J

jazz compositions 16–19
    "Ain't Misbehavin'" 17
    "A-tiskit, A-tasket" 15, 18
    "Black and Tan Fantasy" 16
    "Heebie Jeebies" 12, 16
    "Hello Dolly" 12, 19
    "One O'Clock Jump" 14, 17
    "Sing, Sing, Sing" 13, 18
    "Take Five" 19
jazz performers 12–15
    Armstrong, Louis 7, 10, 12,
       15, 16, 18, 19, 27
    Basie, Count 8, 11, 14, 15, 16,
       17
    Beiderbecke, Bix 10, 12, 16,
       17
    Bilk, Acker 8, 12
    Bolden, Buddy 6, 7
    Brubeck, Dave 11, 14, 18, 19
    Coltrane, John 12, 13, 19
    Davis, Miles 8, 13
    Ellington, Duke 8, 11, 14, 16,
       17, 18, 19

    Fitzgerald, Ella 8, 15, 17, 18
    Getz, Stan 9, 12, 17, 19
    Gillespie, Dizzy 10, 11, 19
    Goodman, Benny 8, 11, 13,
       17, 18
    Holiday, Billie 15, 16, 17
    Joplin, Scott 6
    Krupa, Gene 11
    Marsalis, Wynton 13
    Miller, Glen 8
    Morrison, James 9, 12
    Morton, "Jelly Roll" 6, 7, 14
    Oliver, King 7, 12, 18
    Parker, Charlie "Bird" 8, 10,
       12, 17, 19
    Shaw, Artie 11, 12, 15, 17, 19
    Waller, Fats 11, 14, 17, 18
    Webb, Chick 15, 17, 18
jazz timeline 6–9

K

Kansas City jazz 8

L

Lomax, Alan 22, 26, 29

M

modern jazz 9, 11
music, main elements of 4
musical terms 4

N

New Orleans jazz 7, 12, 15

R

ragtime 6, 9
rhythm and blues 21

S

slavery 6, 22, 30
swing 8, 9, 11, 13, 14, 15, 18
syncopation 5